WHY DO WE CELEBRATE CHRISTMAS?

Holidays Kids Book
Children's Christmas Books

BABY PROFESSOR

EDUCATION KIDS

In this book, we're going to talk about why people around the world celebrate Christmas. So, let's get right to it!

Over 2,000 years ago, a woman gave birth to a baby in a stable. That baby was Jesus Christ and Christians believe that He was and is God who had come to Earth in the form of a man. His mission on Earth was to save all of mankind from their sins so that people could be forgiven and gain everlasting life.

The Nativity of Jesus Christ

The New Testament of the Bible outlines the story of what happened before Jesus was born and after He was born. The birth of Jesus is written about in both the Gospel of Luke and the Gospel of Matthew. The reason that Christians celebrate Christmas is because it is a celebration of the birth of Jesus.

THE CHRISTMAS STORY

Jesus's parents, Mary and Joseph, weren't married yet. They were engaged to be married when Mary was visited by the angel Gabriel. He told her that she would get pregnant by God's miracle. She would have a son and He would be Jesus, the Son of God and the Savior of mankind.

Announcement of the birth of Jesus

Mary was scared, but she believed in God's word so she accepted her role. The angel Gabriel also told her that her cousin Elizabeth, who was considered too old to get pregnant, was going to have a baby too. She would give birth to John the Baptist who would prepare the people to welcome Jesus.

When Joseph found out that Mary was pregnant, he didn't know whether he should marry her anymore. They hadn't been together as man and wife so he didn't understand how she had become pregnant. However, an angel visited Joseph as well to explain the situation to him and to tell him that Mary was carrying God's son. Joseph would be the earthly father of God's son.

Mary and Joseph

Joseph and Mary were married and they soon had to travel from the city of Nazareth to the city of Bethlehem. The Roman Emperor Augustus wanted a complete list of all the people who lived in the Roman Empire so they would pay their taxes. Joseph and Mary had to travel to Bethlehem because this was Joseph's birthplace.

Bethlehem

They had to walk for 70 miles. This was an incredible hardship for a woman who was pregnant and a husband who needed to take care of her and the unborn Son of God. Mary rode on a donkey and Joseph pulled the donkey along. They were traveling slowly and were concerned because Mary would have to deliver the baby soon.

When they got to Bethlehem there was no place for them to stay for the night, so they stayed with the animals in a stable. Mary gave birth to Jesus and wrapped Him in a long piece of cloth called swaddling clothes, which she wrapped tightly around Him. She placed Him in a makeshift bed, which was a manger filled with hay.

In the fields surrounding Bethlehem, shepherds were tending their flocks. Angels came to them to announce the glad tidings of Jesus's birth. The shepherds were initially scared, but when they heard the news that the Savior had been born, they were joyous.

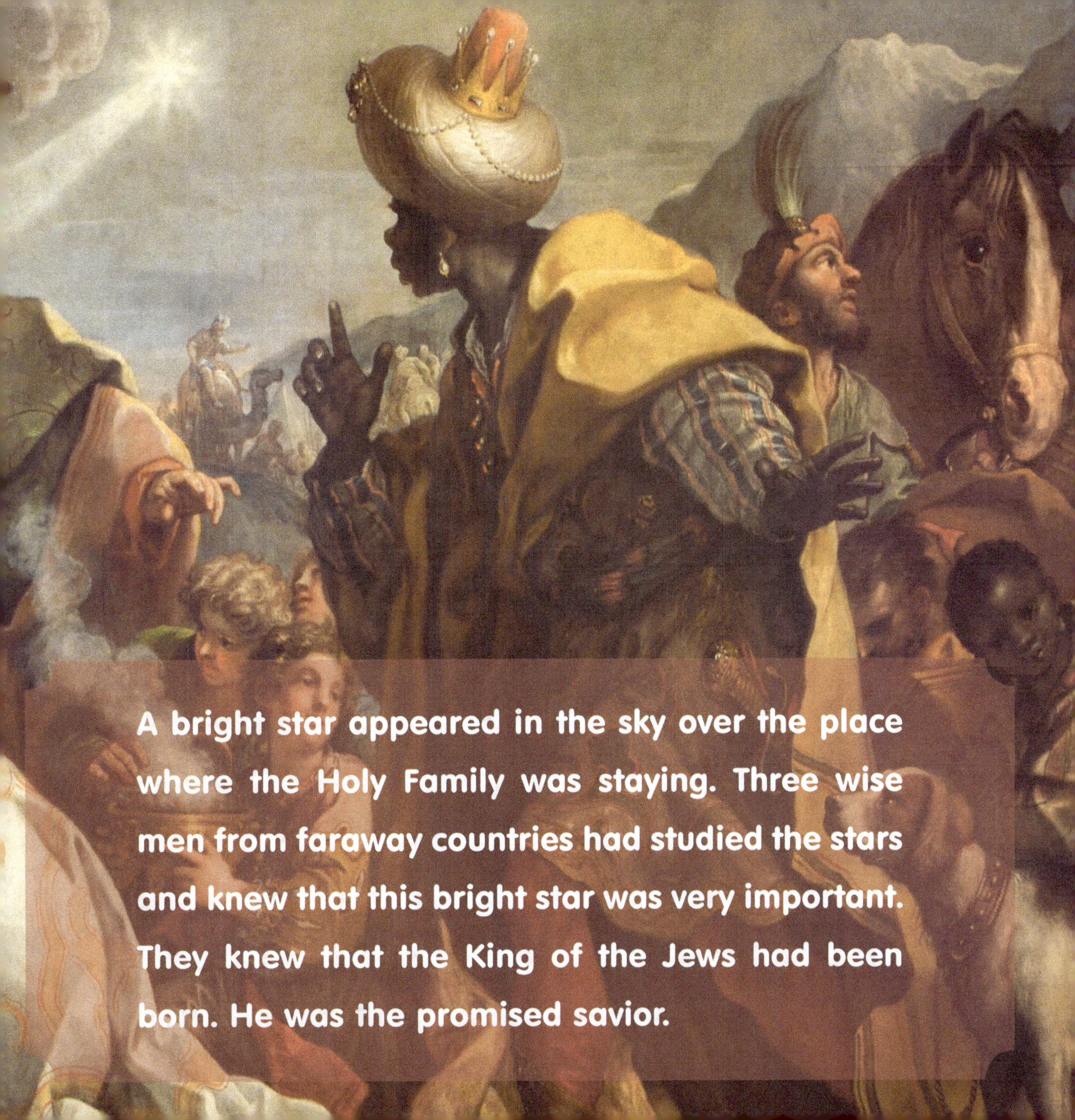

A bright star appeared in the sky over the place where the Holy Family was staying. Three wise men from faraway countries had studied the stars and knew that this bright star was very important. They knew that the King of the Jews had been born. He was the promised savior.

They brought three gifts to the baby.

➭ Gold, which symbolized Jesus's reign as a spiritual king

➭ Frankincense, an incense, which symbolized that He was God as well as man

➭ Myrrh, an embalming oil, which symbolized that He would give His life for mankind

Jesus Christ in the Gethsemane garden

This was the beginning of Christ's life on Earth
that would end in His death on the cross and His
resurrection into heaven.

THE CELEBRATION OF CHRISTMAS

When Christians celebrate Christmas, they are celebrating the birth of Jesus, their Savior. Christians also celebrate to offer peace and good will to others and to let their families and friends know that they are loved by exchanging gifts. The traditions of Christmas are different in every culture and have changed a great deal throughout the centuries.

Pope Julius 1

The Bible doesn't mention the exact day or exact location of Jesus's birth. In fact, in the early days of the Christian religion, Easter, the day for celebrating Christ's resurrection was the major holiday. In the fourth century, the Roman Catholic leaders decided that it would be right to celebrate the Savior's birth. Since the Bible didn't mention an exact date, Pope Julius I decided upon December 25th.

Prior to Christianity a pagan festival called Saturnalia had been celebrated at this time. Saturnalia was a celebration of the pagan god Saturn who was the god of the harvest and agriculture. Historians believe that the pope wanted the Romans to turn their attention away from the wild partying that took place during Saturnalia. Now that they had embraced Christianity and the spirituality that went with it, their holiday celebrations should be more holy.

The Roman Saturnalia

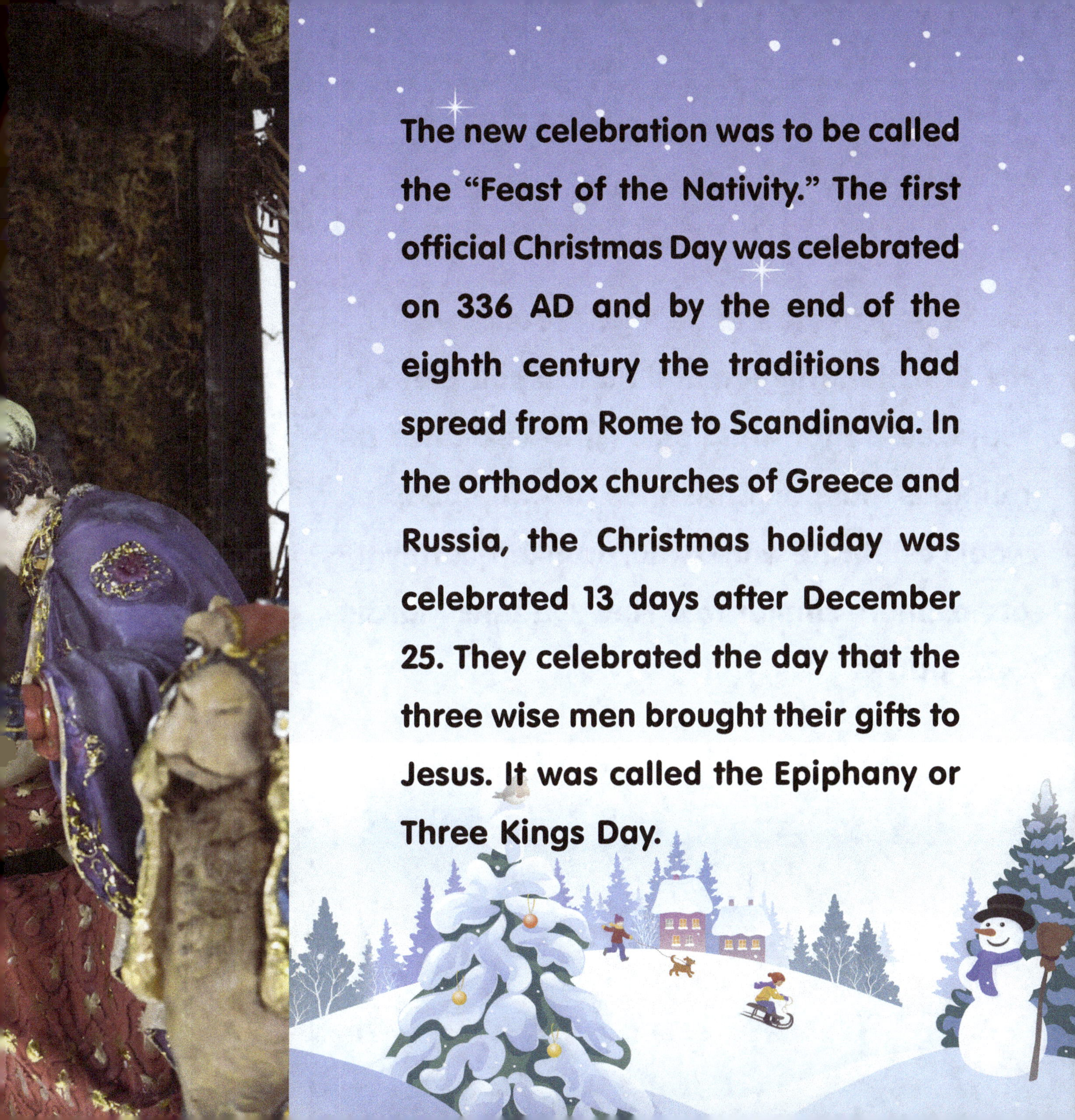

The new celebration was to be called the "Feast of the Nativity." The first official Christmas Day was celebrated on 336 AD and by the end of the eighth century the traditions had spread from Rome to Scandinavia. In the orthodox churches of Greece and Russia, the Christmas holiday was celebrated 13 days after December 25. They celebrated the day that the three wise men brought their gifts to Jesus. It was called the Epiphany or Three Kings Day.

By the time of the Middle Ages around 476 AD, the Christian religion had almost completely replaced pagan religions. However, after a religious mass on Christmas Day, the people would celebrate with a wild, drunken, carnival atmosphere similar to a New Orleans Mardi Gras party.

Christmas Day Celebration

Family celebrating Christmas

Each year, a student or beggar was crowned as the "king of misrule" and would go with his subjects to the houses of the upper class to be given the best food and drink. If the owners of the house didn't comply with the request, they would be terrorized by the lower-class people.

Christmas was celebrated for centuries in Europe. Each country had different traditions. Some countries had Saint Nicholas. Others had Christmas trees decorated with lights. Still others set up Nativity scenes. All of these traditions have been adapted and are still in use today.

CHRISTMAS IN THE UNITED STATES

Although the English had brought their Christmas traditions to the United States, after the colonies broke away from the British, the English traditions weren't followed anymore. Then, in the 19th century things changed. Americans transformed their Christmas traditions from a wild holiday to a peaceful, family tradition filled with love and nostalgia.

In 1819, Washington Irving wrote The Sketchbook of Geoffrey Crayon, Gent. It was a series of short stories about Christmas celebrations that took place in an English manor. In this book, Irving recreated the Christmas holiday the way he thought it should be done with people from different classes sharing their holiday with good food and merriment.

Washington Irving

Washington Irving and his Literary Friends

He presented it as if these were the true traditions although it wasn't based on anything he had actually experienced. One of the short stories in the book was "The Legend of Sleepy Hollow." This story and others made him famous in both England and the United States and new traditions were born.

A CHRISTMAS CAROL

In 1843, Charles Dickens wrote A Christmas Carol. This amazing story about how a man is transformed by his greedy, miserly ways into a giving, generous person as he becomes aware of his folly during the Christmas season forever changed the way that people viewed Christmas. The novel was acclaimed in both the United States and England.

Charles Dickens

Family Opening Christmas Presents

The family structure in the United States was changing too. The needs of children were becoming more important. There was less strict discipline and more loving and nurturing within the home. At Christmas time, parents and relatives could give children gifts without the fear that they would be "spoiling" them or making them unruly.

In 1822, an Episcopal minister by the name of Clement Clarke Moore created a poem for his three daughters. It was eventually called "The Night Before Christmas" and forever changed the ancient view of Saint Nicholas to our modern-day Santa Claus.

Clement C. Moore

Christmas was declared a national holiday in 1870 and Americans began to study and re-invent the traditions of their ancestors and make new ones to create a truly American Christmas. Retailers began to capitalize on the gift-giving traditions of the holiday and today about one-sixth of all retail spending in the United States is for Christmas.

WHY DO NON-CHRISTIANS CELEBRATE CHRISTMAS?

Christmas has become so popular that even non-Christians in the United States still like to celebrate it. Over 80% of the non-Christian population still participates in different aspects of the Christmas holiday.

Family celebrating Christmas

WHY DO WE CELEBRATE CHRISTMAS?

We celebrate Christmas to honor Christ's birth, but we also celebrate in the hopes that all men, women, and children around the world will live in peace and good will with each other. We hope that the traditions of love expressed with gift-giving and celebration will extend out from our families to other families around the world.

Awesome! Now you know more about the reasons why Christians and non-Christians celebrate Christmas. You can find more Christmas books from Baby Professor by searching the website of your favorite book retailer.

Family celebrating Christmas

Visit
BABY PROFESSOR
EDUCATION KIDS
www.BabyProfessorBooks.com
to download Free Baby Professor eBooks
and view our catalog of new and exciting
Children's Books